I Apologize

for Nothing

A Man's Poetry

Jim Melanson

I APOLOGIZE FOR NOTHING
A Man's Poetry

Melanson Publishing,
Newcastle, Ontario
www.melansonpublishing.ca

First Published 2014
ISBN: 978-0-9937565-0-4

Printed by CreateSpace, an Amazon.com Company
Available from Amazon.com and other online stores.

For more information and other titles visit
www.melansonpublishing.ca

To Gaelan, my son.

Never be afraid to cry...

Contents

Preface

When I was a hormone driven teenager, I often put pen to paper. Of the many discarded poetic attempts, there were a few that remained. They were particularly powerful to me at the time. They still are, almost thirty-five years later. I typed them on recycled paper with my mother's old manual Brother Typewriter, tucked them away and then over time, forgot about them.

Fast forward more than enough years and I found myself going through old belongings and coming across those writings. Ironically, I was going through much of the same angst that I had when the old words were first typed, twenty-five years before. Finding these words and reading them with fresh perspective was shocking. I was, at the time of finding them, going through many of the emotions, questions and doubts that had originally led to the teenage poems.

Over the next few years, I found myself with pen on paper again, trying to handle the complexities of emotions that I was going through. It was an unfortunate time once again in my life but I had my health, I had a roof over my head and I had clothes on my back. Life had a much different perspective as to what was needed and what was wanted.

I realized that I was wholly connected with my younger self through thematic experiences that repeated through life. It didn't matter that I had learned a lesson each time. It seemed that God had more for me to learn and He wasn't going to let me skip school.

The writing had helped as a teenager so now as an adult, I put pen to paper again (actually, it was finger tips to keyboard). As I wrote some of the more recent lines you are about to read, I realized that I wasn't only exploring my current state, I was also time travelling with my teenage self. For a brief period of time while writing each of the later poems, I was he and he was me. Young me and mature me were sharing experiences, sharing thoughts, sharing memories, sharing tears, sharing comfort. These experiences gave me hope. I survived before. I will survive again.

I've often been amazed that when someone is in an emotional state, one of the first things they do when they are coming down from that tightrope is to apologize to those around them. Humph. How dare they?

Having spent many years numbed and feeling nothing, I can tell you what a blessing it is to feel anything. The hard things we go through remind us we are feeling, loving creatures. The hard things we go through are the bittersweet counter point that makes the joyful times all that much more joyful. People get embarrassed when others see their emotional states. They become embarrassed or ashamed. I think it's because the vulnerable state of high emotion goes back to our primal selves that, if you believe Jung's "collective unconscious" theory, is shared by all of us.

Vulnerable = Eaten By Bears.

I don't believe a person can truly do "smiles" unless they are willing to risk doing "tears". You have to be able to risk to be able to gain, even if sometimes it is your tenuous grasp on your temporary sanity that is at risk.

As you explore my words, you are going to find some that take you back to your teen years, some words that take you back to painful times. Don't shy away from those memories, even if there are memories of pain and hurt. Those feelings are a valid and important part of you. There are no bears on the street to eat you. Those things you feel have made you who you are today and today, you are perfectly you!

If you are reading this while lost in the depths of that pain, I want to reassure you that you have been here before, you will be here again and you will survive. I did…

…and I apologize for nothing!

A Man's Poetry

Demon Toy

My emotions are but a toy,
Oh, how those demons love to fondle them,
Play till their hearts content,
With tears that are not theirs.

I anguish as I watch them pass,
To know that, that was once my lass,
I hear their conscience say, "I'm sorry my dear",
I see their soul say, "I don't care".

I know I am a fool to write,
What else should I do on this lonely night,
Oh, how I wish my arms could hold,
A bonnie lass, from memories old.

I so vividly recall the day I wrote this, at the manly age of fifteen. My first girlfriend had very gently and compassionately dumped me. I hurt, and it hurt deep. The first person who had found me worthy in my mind, no longer found me worthy. While I knew intellectually that these things happened, it was still my first experience with these emotions and these thoughts.

A short time later, I found out she was dating someone else. I discovered then the confluence of the torpid River of Rejection with the mighty and turbulent River of Pain. It was a place I would return to many times in my life.

I remember sitting alone in my room at night, the lights off, the window open, and the sound of the world outside; while I felt the silence of my tears inside. I felt angry, I felt betrayed and I felt foolish. I tried not to cry, because it made me feel weak and foolish. I also remember feeling that no one could see me, so it was okay. There were no bears in my room.

Fast forward a few years, and I went through an almost identical experience. I was nineteen, she was seventeen. She was beautiful, fun, and charismatic. At nineteen, I sat on the edge of the bed one day, held in my mother's arms, crying without shame for the pain. There are some days in life when you just need Mom to hug you.

Looking back on this now, thirty years later, I have such compassion for that young man. I'm a lot tougher now. I have the strength of experience, self-confidence and a positive self-image. Still, I have to extend a warm embrace back to that younger me. If I could truly travel through time I would just wrap my arms around him, hold him silently and let him cry until the hot tears came no more.

If only I had the ability to cry now. I haven't cried for myself, for any reason, since my ex-wife and I separated ten years ago…

Consumption

The blackness covered me like a blanket,
It was cold and musty,
I turned and ran,
I could not see where I was going,
I heard something,
It was behind me,
I could not see it,
It was too dark,
The echoing footsteps,
Behind me again,
I could not make it,
I was tiring,
The blackness covered me like a blanket.

This was a teenager's fear manifest. Fear of being rejected, fear of being laughed at, and fear of always being alone; because he would never "fit in" with the people he so badly wanted to fit in with. Now, thirty-plus years later, I embrace that young fellow who still lives inside me. Still a geek, still a nerd, still a bit "odd" or "different"- I find it hard to make friends. The friends I do make though, I am committed to.

I was raised in a tough environment. Not tough like drugs, booze, or homelessness, etc. It was tough emotionally. As a young child I rarely found anything was "good enough". I kept striving to do better, to make sure I was loved. As a child I would stand lost for words or the ability to act: wringing my hands, my heart pounding, bordering on hyperventilating. What did I have to do to be perfect? What did I have to do to be a good little boy? What did I have to do not to be yelled at? What did I have to do not to be hit? What did I have to do to be loved?

My mother loved me. This I knew and know to this day. At the time of life when I went through these things, she was going through a very difficult time of her own. As I look back, I know that nothing I went through warranted those responses, but being a child of five and six at the time, I didn't know that and didn't have a roadmap to follow.

Years later, as a teenager and making new friends, I found myself in those old trances - but for different reasons and for different people. I was a geek, I was a nerd, and I had no confidence. I had a weird sense of humour, I wanted so desperately to fit in and for people to like me, and I wanted so desperately to be enough for others. When I was thirteen I was lucky enough to find myself in the Air Cadets (527 Simonds). I loved the structure; I loved how rigid the program was, and the fact that there were no assessments of how nerdy I was. Eventually, I started making friends there; friends that were as weird and nerdy as I was. Some of those friend-ships have lasted a life time.

The angst and fears of that young man became tools that I used for myself. From time to time, in new situations, new workplaces, new living environments and new romances. I used the feelings that triggered those fears to be a coach's whistle telling me it was time to step up and be strong. The way we become strong is by being strong. The way we become confident, is by being confident. The way we change and become more, is by being responsible for ourselves.

If I said I didn't need that coach's whistle anymore, I would by lying. However, I use it for a different reason now. In my younger years I used that alert to help me conform and be more like others. Now in my life I use that coach's whistle to let me know when I am being too conformist, when I am selling myself out, or when I am being less than who I know I am.

If you are a teenager reading this and you understand or maybe feel the same fears, let me tell you what is most important. When it comes to having positive experiences, fun and non-destructive good times, or forming positive and lasting relationships, what is most important is taking a chance. Like Nike says, "Just Do It."

Don't sit back and let the fear control you. Accept the fear, embrace it: because it is a raw emotion that you can USE as a tool for yourself.

Yes, some people are going to reject you, some people are not going to find you interesting. That's okay. There will be lots of people you encounter, that will not be your cup of tea either. As that geeky, fear disabled child, I can tell you that my life has taught me that for every one person who rejected me or didn't find me "good enough" for their "crowd", who didn't find me their "cup of tea", there were at least TEN other people who accepted and welcomed me with open arms, open hearts and without conditions.

Be strong.

BE YOU!

Memories of You

As the twilight hours nighly approach,
And darkness is my veil,
I crawl down deep into my sleep,
And await my thoughts to prevail.

As the hours are born,
Of early morn',
I turn away to see,
Those memories old,
Come take hold,
And reveal my life – to me.

They dig down deep,
And bring to me,
The memories I wish to suppress,
The torment I know,
That will take hold,
As I slowly cause their unrest.

They lay before me – so innocent,
And then they begin to unfold,
And as I was told,
By a young man of old,
They feel like a knife in my chest.

I see the people I know,
Though their time has come to pass,
But, oh, how I long,
For them to return,
To touch,
To hold,
To caress.

I say to myself, "You fool!",
Don't incarnate those old wounds,
They hurt too much,
You subconscious slut,
My life, holds for them,
No more room.

But alas I lose,
The battle is won,
I long for a tender touch,
I look to you,
And I feel you move,
So I know that we are still one.

My memories grow fogged,
My alarm awakes,
I feel your love in my heart,
I look forward to my sleep,
Cause I know what keeps,
In the silent memories of the dark.

This poem was born of bed time tears, a lack of sleep and the treasured comfort of dreams that filled my mind when I did finally find unconsciousness. This was written a few weeks after Demon Toy, the first poem in this book. Thoroughly unequipped to deal with the feelings I had back then, I found sleep to be a devious solace. Too many nights of only two or three hours sleep. When I did sleep, images of my first teenage love filled my dreams. Writing this poem turned out to be a catharsis for my pain.

We use to hold Wake-a-Thons to raise money for our Air Cadet Squadron. I remember writing this particular poem at three a.m. in the morning, sitting on top of a desk in a room by myself. People kept poking their head in the doorway to see what I was doing; so I lied about it of course.

Whether it was the sleep deprivation of the Wake-a-Thon or the release these prose gave me, the day I returned home I slept like a not quite so innocent baby.

Of course, I dreamt of her.

Unfortunately, twenty plus years later I found myself going through an identical experience, a repeat. My wife and I had separated, and while I thought I was ready to deal with it, I wasn't. It was during that suffering that I came upon these writings, and so powerfully re-connected across time with my teenage self.

The Love I Never Had

I scream a silent scream,
I feel no fear,
I feel no love,
My heart begs for a gentle touch,
A crimson moment of passion,
A mutual amour.

"Why?" I appeal to my creator,
Why must I suffer alone with myself?
Why do I fear love?

I have none to lose,
I have all to gain,
I love those I love,
I love those I hate,
Yet, I love no one!

Well, this one is just chock full o' stuff!

On the first glance it's about a teenager who can't get a girlfriend. Digging deeper, we see many more things. We also see the silent screaming rage memory of a child who never knew real, honest, unconditional love from his mother.

The morning of the day that my father died, he and I had "words" and parted with me storming out of the house in adolescent indignation; slamming the door behind me and cussing him under my breathe. That last scene with my father drove a lot of the pain in this entry, *"I love those I love, I love those I hate."*

I wrote this when I was someone who did not know how to love - and I knew I did not know how to love - and I was terrified that I was never going to learn what real love was. I was horrified at the prospect that I would forever be left wanting, at the bakery window, with no change in my pocket.

Thirty years later, I'm single again. I've been on my own for ten years now. After all this time, I once again find myself standing at the bakery window, with no change in my pocket. The only difference is that now I'm no longer sure I want to open the bakery door, even though sometimes, my mouth still waters.

The Grim Reaper

You aged grapes of Rome,
Fermented since the Ides of March,
How bitter thou nectar tastes,
How sweet thou nectar lies...

I curse thy lonely presence and
How stealthily you visit at night,
Your harvest is a single term,
Thou catholic scythe is honed to life.

The pity of harvest is memories,
The scent of ages gone by,
We curse your legal intrusion,
Yet welcome your hasty good-bye.

This poem was inspired by Shakespeare's Julius Caesar (for the imagery); however, it was written about my father's death.

The first line, "*You aged grapes of Rome*," embodies my childhood view of how old my father was, death itself and the sweet irony that growing up means gain and loss. Wine is nice. Older wine is better. However, at some point, given enough years, wine will poison itself.

The microbes in the fermentation process consuming the sugars that release the alcohol-ethanol as a by-product will eventually succumb to the ethanol itself: turning the wine back into vinegar. That fact that what is created eventually destroys its creator, made me think of the many times I had disappointed my Dad and the times we had fought. The reality is, my Dad and I got along great and loved each other deeply. However, at the time of his death, our thoughts are always focused on the morbidity of the moment, in all its nefarious forms.

Moving along those thought lines; this poem is about the bitter irony of death. Bitter in how it leaves those behind in pain, "*How bitter thou nectar tastes*". But also sweet in that it will end suffering and allow a person to be reborn as a renewed spirit in the everlasting glory of God. In this poem the word "catholic" (small 'c') refers to the universal and blind nature of deaths swinging scythe. The reference to the Ides of March (Et To Brute?) brings about the feeling that death, on the surface, is the highest form of betrayal by life itself, or, so it would seem to be a betrayal "*How sweet thou nectar lies...*"

If a person could take only one thing from this poem, I would hope they take and hold dear the line "*Your harvest is a single term.*" There are no do-overs. If we get it wrong, we don't get to re-spawn at a saved reset point. You don't have to do it right the first time, but keep doing it until you get it right. Don't ever leave anything unsaid. There are so many things left unsaid to my father. The very last time he saw me, I was grousing at him, turning my back on him, slamming the door in his face.

I can't count the times over the years that morning's "final act" in his life has brought tears to my eyes, and the deepest of aching regrets to my heart. If only I could have that do-over. There are so many things I want to say to him, so many things I needed to ask him. So many times I needed his mentoring, his guidance, and his advice. I would never have those things. I would never be able to tell him I didn't think that he was an ass and that I loved him with every breath I took. The Grim Reaper had intruded. For me, there was never a hasty good bye. It took seventeen years for me to finally deal with my father's death, but even now, sitting here typing these words, I feel the hot burn of tears welling behind my eyelids.

My spiritual formation allows me to have no fear of death. The day will be amazing when I go home to God's glory. That doesn't mean I'm actively seeking the day to arrive any sooner than God intends, but I've become comfortable with the thought of my own passing (hopefully a great many years away). Still, I've lost too many friends and family over the years to become comfortable with the loss of those I love.

His Presence

O, my Christian soul,
Mentor and friend, through
Love and tribulations,
Darkened to no presence,
Wary of all.

Harken my regressions, O
Carrier of my soul,
Enlighten my presence,
Make me not salt.

Eden of my life,
Cain of my sin,
Crutch thee my life,
Make haste to my den.

When I was a teenager and young adult, I bounced around between religions, trying to find a source of enlightenment, love, safety, faith, etc. I kept looking everywhere, as most people do, for God, Jesus, some faith, and safety.

What I didn't realize was that it was there all the time. God was waiting for me. I just had to acknowledge Him. I just had to open my heart and invite him in.

For a great deal of my life, I turned my back on God and religion. I lived many dark and scary things. I was involved in the occult, witchcraft and many other dark practices. Eventually, thankfully, my best friend saved my life. She turned to me one day when I was going through a particularly hard time and said, "Maybe it's time to let go, and let God."

I gave my life over to God that day. I opened my heart, confessed my sins, acknowledged my weakness and asked God to take the reins in my life. Since then, life has been so amazingly better! Especially in these last few years as I have learned more about God and formed a relationship through prayer with our Lord and Saviour, Jesus. My life has been truly amazing.

The final two lines seems to sum up the loss and yearning for redemption, salvation, and freedom that I needed, "*Crutch thee my life, Make haste to my den.*"

Dustbunnies

Dustbunnies, dustbunnies,
Vacuum, sweep, wipe and pluck,
Company is coming,
My house is not in order.

The lamp was extinguished,
I saw the walls need repairing,
Filled the cracks with polyfil but
Can see they need replacing.

A fresh coat of paint,
Would make my home bright and airy,
The foundation, however,
Needs prep, plaster and working.

Dusbunnies, dustbunnies,
Making a mess of my space,
Lurking in corners just out of sight,
Always hiding, waiting and lying in wait.

Cute little whisps of days gone by,
The dustbunnies now just mess my space,
Once they were cute and kept me entertained,
Now they obscure and rend my peace.

It's time to do some spring cleaning,
Release the dustbunnies I hold,
Let go of the clutter,
Let go of the mess.

Say good bye to the dustbunnies,
Say goodbye to the past,
Say good bye to the mess,
Say hello to the next.

This poem was written in July 2004, not long after my 39th birthday. I was unhappy with a lot of things in my life. My relationships, how I looked, how I felt about my world, the place I lived, etc. My ex-wife and I had separated six months prior; and I was now living in a new apartment, on my own, for the first time ...in a LONG time.

I always get hit hard when I read the line, "*The lamp was extinguished*". The events surounding this time in my life caused me to take a good hard look at myself and realize how truly unhappy I was about so many things. I realized I was unhappy because I had simply lost that oh-so-important positive self-image. Once again, alone and love snatched from my petulant grasp, I was feeling I had been found unworthy.

It was after much introspection and calling on the present lessons, plus the lessons of previous loves and life, that I realized I had not been found unworthy at all. It was simply a matter that she had changed and I had changed - and we were no longer the people who met and fell in love. While love was, and is still present in my heart, we no longer shared the same vision of the future; we no longer shared the same dreams, we were no longer "simpatico".

This poem was acknowledgement that I had a lot of work to do, but that it was wholly work on myself. My self-esteem, my self-image, my faith, my confidence and my belief in myself populated that particular work manifest. I realized that there would be no way I was going to be able to form a new relationship with anyone until I had done the work for myself, to learn to love myself again, first.

Company is coming, my house is not in order. Gotta love the allegory.

Raindrops

The sun sets on the purple horizon,
Cast adrift, the water lily sails,
Withers,
Raindrops splash upon my cheeks.

A great rushing of air fills my lungs,
Held and hoarded it nourishes my corpse,
Pointlessly,
Raindrops splash upon my cheeks.

Shrieks of laughter and love are memories,
The compass bears south-south-east,
Reckoning,
Raindrops splash upon my cheeks.

Fury and madness tear me quietly,
Impotent futility steals my dreams,
Mercilessly,
Raindrops splash upon my cheeks.

Too much as too little,
Unmercifully I am Damocles,
Late,
Raindrops splash upon my cheeks.

A supplication offered to the Raven,
Bargaining with the rule of three,
Insanity,
Raindrops splash upon my cheeks,

The hand of inspiration and eternity,
Goes silently from mine,
Gifting,
Raindrops splash upon my cheeks.

The bitter rot in my soul permeates my mind,
The bitter root tastes ... bitter,
Agony,
Raindrops splash upon my cheeks.

How let go of my life's bounty,
How scream for my hearts Sunshine,
Painfully,
Raindrops splash upon my cheeks,

My perfect passion and my perfect grace,
This one word can never pass my lips,
Goodbye,
Raindrops splash upon my cheeks.

This was written not too long after Dustbunnies. As I was getting my house in order for company, I had to spend some time reflecting on the recent end of my marriage and our six years together. Six years that seemed like a lifetime, which seemed like it would never end. She was perfect. She was the one. My pet name for her was Sunshine.

Then we changed. We grew apart.

When we are going through the agony of shattering, the first stage of abandonment, we feel like we will do and surrender anything to rewind time to when it was good, *"A supplication offered to the Raven."* We know that is not possible. Poe's Raven keeps telling us, "Nevermore, Nevermore." We are compelled to try and barter. Simply because of the precarious position we are in, especially when the twisted emotions of our mind think there may be hope; we think perhaps there is one thing we could have done different, said or changed about ourselves. Somehow, the magic panacea will make everything right again (*impotent futility steals my dreams*). Once you have reached that state, doing too much is just as bad as previously having done too little (*too much as too little*). Nothing will change that feeling of damned if you do, damned if you don't (*unmercifully I am Damocles*). Once you get there, almost always, it is too late (*Late*).

My ex was the one. She was the one that was supposed to last forever. She was my own "it" girl. Letting go of her was like having the fabric of my reality ripped from my fingers, like having my heart and sense of reality rent by the merciless illogic of Agares.

I went through a deep dark hell with the end of that relationship, my third marriage. There were days when the tears simply wouldn't stop, when I would find myself curled up on the floor with a tear sodden shirt. I thought, for a time, that I was going to go mad. Slowly, day by day, I got hold of myself and reached a point where I could function. Truthfully, it was years before I got over her. Sitting here a little over ten years later, I can say without hesitation that I finally did get over Sunshine.

I never said that I stopped loving her...

Breathe

My senses awaken to the flow of the universe,
Suddenly, I'm sitting across from you,
Then realizing that it was I, really I,
Who made the steps to be there.

Wafting memories, my days clouded in fantasy,
Emotional jetsam, dreams blended with reality,
Quiet yearning, a return to a lovers embrace,
Shattered beliefs, new found faith.

I watch your lips move with fluid feminine grace,
Dancing the tango of words that reveal you,
The true you comes forth in unexpected honesty,
So well acquainted with yourself.

Hungrily listening, seeking my breadths,
Consuming quiet, measuring my depths,
Intense gaze, your eyes explore my soul,
Open acceptance, true desire to know my all.

Base representations of materialism don't arrive,
Sharing your faults and pains astounds me,
You are human and you hurt and you bleed,
So uncommon is this raw display of truth.

Hopeful gazes, a future not empty,
Faith restored, a vision of what could be,
Be brave, life and laughter and love are worth it,
Maybe you, maybe not.

My breath slows and my heart quickens,
We seem to blend as one without touching,
Union of fantasy, reality, hope and faith,
Breathe....

This one is a tribute, if you will, to faith and belief in the future. This is a poem about no one in particular. It was written about eight years ago during a mental vay-kay. Also, the energy of this particular entry is quite different. It's written not so much as a wish, rather, as a prayer. Philippians 4:6 (NIV) says, "Do not be anxious about anything, but in every situation, by prayer and petition, with thanksgiving, present your requests to God."

As I went through the healing process of the end of my third marriage in 2004, I started to face the reality that at some point, I would have to start dating again. I knew it was a future consideration. I certainly was not ready to start dating then.

At that time I needed to shut out the hurting things, the emotions, regrets and absent solace that I had been going through. I took a mental sojourn forward to what I thought would be the greatest first-date ever. I hoped that I would meet the one that would last a lifetime (finally). I hoped I would meet someone that would simply accept me as me, without expectation, without the need to change me.

At the time, I had an ideal for the perfect first date. It would be having a picnic with a person worth the effort, near the water. A blanket, transistor radio, homemade food (I love to cook!), and a sunny day. Two people, seemingly so mismatched, taking the time - through the bravery of their heart and soul, to get to know and learn about each other, through honest communication. They have the need to seek and understand the real person before them: un-fettered by the trappings of public restaurants, with ease and grace they cast off all pretensions, all masquerades. Their soul desire is to find out if they have what it takes to be with each other.

Instead, what I found over the following years were women who judged and laughed at me. One woman even told me she agreed to meet for drinks just so she could see what kind of loser had been married three times. Oddly, I still believe. I still have faith that love is a possibility. *Union of fantasy, reality, hope and faith. Breathe...*

Masquerade

Painted faces, crying in their love,
Torn together,
Joined apart,
Masquerade, Masquerade.

Pious reflections, revocation of honesty,
All lies,
No truth,
Masquerade, Masquerade.

Dreams of lies, hopes glistened with sorrow,
Be honest,
Don't hide,
Masquerade, Masquerade.

Fear, sometimes, masquerades as love,
I love them so much,
I can never leave,
Masquerade, Masquerade.

Painted faces, shattered in the light,
See your truth,
Respect yourself,
Masquerade, Masquerade.

Reality was sinking in about love. Reality was revealing the true nature of many things to me. I looked back at past relationships and things I had learned about relationships in general. Duplicity and the contrary nature of how we avoid seeing our own weaknesses abound through this offering.

We all wear masks. We have our work mask, our commuter mask, our partners mask, our as-a-parent mask, our as-a-child mask, our friends mask, our neighbour mask, our shopping-at-the-store mask, our confidant mask, our victim mask, our self-defense mask, our church mask, our party mask, our looking in the mirror mask ... the list is endless.

We spend so much time wearing all these masks ... does it seem surprising we have a hard time knowing ourselves? Does it seem surprising we have a hard time knowing those around us? It's truly amazing the amount of things we keep to ourselves, that we should be sharing with that one most important person in our lives. Sometimes the most powerful knocking on our vanity door is the knock of our loves' gaze. Of all the people in the world we want to be perfect for, we wind up putting on a mask with the one we should be prostrating ourselves before in abject honesty. We do this with our children. We do this with our parents. We do this with our partners. We even, sometimes, try to do this with God.

"*Fear, sometimes, masquerades as love,*" is an observation that I have made too many times in myself and in others. How many times has an abused woman rejected the appeal to leave him because she reasons, "But I love him" or the ever discouraging, "but deep down he really loves me". What is it? Is it love? Is it fear of being alone? Is it fear of feeling no one finds us worthy?

Which is worse? Being in a bad relationship or feeling that no one wants to be in a relationship with us? If you have to ask that question of yourself, you are wearing your, "looking in the mirror mask."

My marriage with Sunshine ended ten years ago. I've dated four times since then, now I don't. I realized that those people who rejected me, those women who laughed at me, those people did not have the view and vision of me that I had developed. The lessons Sunshine taught me gave me strength. Those lessons have given me the opportunity to explore who I was, and who I truly am. She had stripped away all the pretentions, she had stripped away all the lies I told myself about myself, she had stripped away all the masquerade masks I tried to wear when looking in the mirror.

When Sunshine took herself out of my life, she gave me back myself. She gave me the greatest gift I have ever received, second only to the blood price Jesus paid for my salvation.

It has been said that people change in relationships. This is to be expected of everyone. New input, new experiences, the things we learn, the things we go through: these all change us. What may be unexpected is how we change. It's unexpected because we don't truly show a person who we are to begin with. They have no expectation of the dramatic upheavals we go through as we slowly, one at a time, peel back the layers of who we are, as we start shedding the masks that we wear.

Sunshine was a relationship of pure love. I thought about past relationships based on love, and relationships based on fear. I thought about all the things I was learning about myself, and about being honest with myself. I thought about how many people are in relationships based on love, and how many more are in relationships based on fear (e.g. of being alone, of being unable to cope alone, of being financially dependent, etc.). So many relationships would be richer, stronger, perhaps survive longer, if we would all just cast our masks aside and allow our partner in life to see who we truly are.

Rather than being afraid of how those around us are changing, perhaps we should embrace and rejoice in the wings of freedom we are giving them to shed their masks.

Absentee Mercy

Resting my head on your soft firm shoulder,
My cheek against your breast,
Strong delicate fingers,
Stroking my temple,
Holding my face.

I thought that I had met you and you were mine,
How bitter to find out I was wrong,
Rending of my hearts beats,
Screaming inside,
Where are you?

An explosion of confusion, rampant in angst,
Sudden separation of the senses,
Adrift and cast upon life,
All alone in the crowd,
Crying with the flies.

Hold me and laugh with me and tease me,
Gaze into my eyes with twinkle and shine,
Soft, moist lips closing on mine,
Shared heart beats,
Shared nights.

The road is lonely and dust gets in my eyes,
I know that life has destined us,
I can hear your heart beating,
Patience, hope, faith,
Where are you?

Sudden separation of the senses, a feeling every one of us has encountered in that moment when we realize the love we have committed ourselves to, body and mind, is fleeing us. Believing that there is still someone out there to share my life with, this poem was written years after Sunshine and I separated.

I had let go. I thought that I was well into healing and had great hope, faith and belief in the future. I also believed that God had another great love in store for me, someone who I was going to make and share an amazing connection with. Still, at the time I was VERY lonely and VERY much missing soft, intimate, passionate touches. I'm a touch person, I love to touch and I love to be touched. Not having someone in my life to share physical contact with is something that, while I deal with, is still quite hard. Unfortunately, the yearning I have for the touch of intimacy (not the same as sex) has led me to a point where touch that is not intimate, is repulsive. I actually don't like touching people at this stage in my life. I like even less, being touched by people. Every innocuous touch of strangers counterpoints too deeply and harshly the absence of the touch of intimacy.

I miss there being someone around to share the day to day routine of life with. I miss there being someone whom I can communicate with, even if only a glance or a touch. Someone who will get silly with me just for the shits n' giggles of it. I miss the intimacy of someone to share both trivial and meaningful pillow talk with, deep into the night.

Ten years later, this is still my Siren song to the one who is yet to come. I can feel her. I can hear her heart beating. I'm just waiting now for God to cross our paths.

Reconstruction

Crashing tides of despair debilitate my mind,
So completely lost, so completely alien,
Torn apart from the inside out,
I have completely lost all sense and faculty,
I am one with nothing, I am nothing, nothing.

So sudden and sweeping is the swath of destruction,
Leaving no vestiges of my former perceptions intact,
This Dark Night descended with a crashing silence,
The stillness of its arrival terrified me,
St. John, be good to me.

I look around at the bitter pieces of my former self,
Molecular deconstruction of my heart, soul and ego,
Completely bereft of cover, there is nothing to hide behind,
My Id shines raw demanding gratification,
Reconstruction of the truth and not the lies, not the lies.

Reconstruction one molecule, one heartbeat at a time,
The true me scares me, my darkness comes to light,
The Old Gentleman of Gehenna walks in my garden,
Selfish, self-centered, self-aggrandizement,
Trying to be more than he, more than I.

A lifetime of disappointments,
Feelings of unworthiness and want,
Bad little boy, you don't love mommy,
Prostitution of the true self for acceptance,
I stand at the bakery window with no change.

To be rather than to seem,
Find the child inside me,
Embrace the child's tears,
Recognizing childish power,
I give him power no more.

One belief at a time,
Finding who I am,
Rescuing me,
Resurrecting me,
Reconstructing me.

I am not who I thought I should be, I am me,
Halting the worry of other people's perceptions,
Their vision is theirs and will only detriment me,
I am not they, they are not I,
I am I, I am I, I am I.

Look beyond the ego's domination, balancing act,
So strong the instant appeasement lies to me,
How quickly it builds sand castles below the high tide line,
So pretty, so beautiful, so complimentary, so real,
High tide leaves me wanting, castles washed away.

Look at me, all selfish and free,
The honesty of my hedonism liberates me,
Life is not just about the journey,
Life is about journeying well,
I demand a smile for each moment of me.

Finally I emerge, my cocoon is my new found love of me,
My wings spread as I finally see that all I was, I am,
My spirit soars as I see I have become the gestalt of me,
Miraculously, by being less than I perceived I need to be,
I am just me, honest me, jubilee!

Whenever I read Reconstruction, I want to jump up and down with joy! If you have read the other poems and notes preceding this offering, you will see elements or themes from all of them in this poem. Reconstruction is a celebration and an affirmation, of the growth, change and healing that I have journeyed through.

I thought my last two relationships were the final blow. I thought they would utterly destroy all that I was. When Sunshine and I parted, I went through a deep, dark hell for a long time. I quite likened it to St. John's Dark Night of the Soul.

My world crashed around me, my love was leaving. The woman who was supposed to be "the one" had grown down a different path than I had grown down. It wasn't her fault. It wasn't my fault. It just was what it was. There was no going back. There has never been any going back. The emptiness, at the time, was a chasm that I thought I would never cross. The fact I had done so, had crossed similar chasms, many times before, meant nothing. When Sunshine and I parted ways, I simply didn't want to go on any more. It took a long, long time to get back to a place where I did want to go on.

From the time of the crash and descent into nothingness, it took me many years to finally put myself back together again, to finally reconstruct myself. How did I know I was there? I fell again one night, I fell into the darkness and despair as though it were saying to me, "Look bonehead, this is where you were, look at where you are now!" By the next day I finally realized that after all the time that had passed, my Dark Night was complete, and I had been reborn a child of life. I was intent on journeying and intent on journeying well.

"*I look around at the bitter pieces of my former self,*" this line is referring to the litter of masks I had stripped away and left smashed on the floor, metaphorically, around my feet. I realized all the lies I had told myself over the years, all the lies I had tried to make a reality for those around me.

"*The Old Gentleman of Gehenna walks in my garden,*" is a reference to Satan, to the destructive power of the illusions we continue to allow ourselves to believe as our own realities. In his book, "The Gospel of

Gehenna Fire", Hermann Neander (1885) writes, "By the cross, 'the old man' is put to death, 'the new man' lives". While this is in reference to the death of the Adam-life and the re-birth of our Jesus-life, the principal of death and resurrection or abandonment of the masks and revelation of our true selves, is allegorically valid.

The fourth and sixth stanzas in this poem are intertwined. South of Jerusalem is the Valley of Hinnom, where, before Christ, children were sacrificed to the pagan god Moloch. "For this reason the valley was deemed to be accursed, and "Gehenna" therefore soon became a figurative equivalent for "hell" (Jewish Encyclopedia: Gehenna, 1906). In my growth and change, I had to sacrifice the safety and security of my masks, of my false beliefs about myself. I had to realize that the formative "safety" perceptions I had formed in my younger years were no longer valid and could no longer have sway or control over me. I had to kill off those old beliefs and ways of thinking; the ways and thinking of the child.

I begin the sixth stanza by hanging a lantern on this. In the sixth stanza, "*To be rather than to seem,*" was my high school motto. Properly, the motto was Esse Quam Videri. While my days at St. Malachy's High School weren't always rainbows and roses, those days greatly contributed to who I am today. Those words, Esse Quam Videri, I have carried with me through all of my adult life and I apply them every single day. Be real. Be true. No masks, no masquerade, don't revoke the honesty of yourself.

The last two stanzas are about the change. It is about me as the Pheonix, about me as the butterfly. This is the re-birth, this is the emergence. This is the me I have been waiting to be. This is really me now. *I am just me, honest me, Jubilee!*

White Knuckle Rider

The future lies before me enticing and scary,
Uncertain honesty and high hopes I carry,
I close my eyes and brace for the ride,
Screaming inside, screaming inside.

Winds of change blow fearfully across my face,
Setting a high bar - I tighten my laces,
God give me strength to seek what I seek,
Do not let me surrender at a time I am weak.

Perfection is an elusive property to quest,
Found it once but now I have to weed the rest,
I cry inside for I know not where this life goes,
Destiny and mission will bring smiles or woes.

Karma is the great leveler of playing fields,
Contracts abound, nothing to use as a shield,
I'm scared in my bravery, happy in my fear,
I quest smiles and laughter but what if I find tears?

I demand the perfect life, does it exist?
Must I adjust and concede, give up on my list?
Do I hold on tight, petulant and demanding?
Do I let go and accept, take what I'm not asking?

The fear wells inside me as I ponder myself,
Do I have the heart for this journey, this hell?
Is it all my own making, am I just afraid?
These questions, damn questions, enough I say.

My life is my life and no one else's,
I am in control and cannot relax it,
I must brace the mainsail and tighten the sheets,
Coil up the lines, then tack and beat.

I must face the aloneness over the settling,
I can only be true to the one I'm protecting,
Maybe I'm selfish, maybe I'll falter,
I guess I am - the white knuckle rider.

Arguably, I saved the best one for last. This is my life saver. When I now have hard days, when I feel the loneliness or have a case of the gloomies, I think of the line, *"I guess I am - the white knuckle rider."*

This poem reflects a time in life or state of mind, if you've ever been there, that can be kind of scary ... but scary in a good way. It's about the fear of the unknown and what is going to happen to us. The internalization stage of the abandonment recovery process is when the downward spiral starts to turn around and move upwards. However, we are conflicted and torn further because there is a part of us that is still stuck in the shattering and withdrawal, while another part that is starting to open an eye and look towards the future (not always in a favourable light).

However, the future, no matter how daunting or scary it may be, is exciting! We come from a place of pain and hurt, seeking the sweet release of joy and happiness. So much potential for change, yet - so much potential for pain. The point of White Knuckle Rider is about making choices. Not about the different choices to make, but about actually making choices. Just do it. Just make a choice. It may be a good choice or it may be a bad choice - but either way, it's better than making no choice and thus, making no movement away from the pain.

For those of you who are living the above (and I have lived it as well), take my hand and squeeze tightly. Show me the strength and the tenacious grip of your very own white knuckles. Let me see your white knuckles as you ride with me. Look me in the eye, and promise to continue the journey but also promise me that you will journey well...

...and to hell with the Bears! Apologize for nothing!

About The Author

Poet, programmer, procrastinator, sci-fi geek, coffee snob, actor and writer.

I'm a man who's made it this far with my sanity mostly intact. Life can be many things and often, as the old Chinese curse says, provides us with interesting times. I have a positive outlook on that interesting life. I have a profound faith in God and strive to live Jesus words every day. I possess the ability to hunch my shoulders at life's slings and arrows while saying, "Meh....WhatEv..."

I love the creative side of life but can't draw a straight line. I love acting but don't act anymore. I've been on stage, on TV and in a movie. Numerous times I was in local theatre stage productions (all amateur) and loved, loved, LOVED being in the spotlight, in front of the crowd and breathing the freedom of the anonymity my characters gave me.

I've spent most of my adult life, as the phenom Canadian rock band BTO put it, "Takin' care of business". I always put work, obligations and others first. Now in my life, on the short side of 50 and seeing where all that has gotten me, I am pursuing the things that I enjoy. Mainly, writing. I have a lot of stories in me to tell and want to tell them in my unique way. Of course, most of those stories involve space ships, hot alien women and cool ray guns. Not all though.

The first work I am publishing is a book of poetry. It took thirty-five years to write it as it spans the related and intertwined emotional experiences of a child and an adult. Soon to follow will be a stage play I wrote ten years ago but am just now putting out into the world. It's about a man who loses his mother and then reflects on the journey with her to make some startling discoveries. Next up on the stage, still in the writing stage and darn, it's going to be good, is a sci-fi novel set on Mars.

I leave east of Toronto in a trailer park, disappointed that I can't find Julian, Ricky or Bubbles anywhere. I live with my life partner and amour, Cleo, my cat. My son is in U of Guelph studying to be a genetic research scientist. I'm single, happy, foot-loose and following my dreams!

Upcoming Titles

Mama's Slippers

This is a play in two acts. Even though it is a stage script, it is a compelling read and will leave you reching for the kleenex.

This is the story about a man who as an adult, finally comes to terms with and understand the woman he loved first. Taking place on the night of her death, the play uses flash backs, narrative and visual devices to convey not only the story, but the heartfelt emotions of the story as well.

What makes this play unique is that every word of it is true. While I've composed a few scenes and events and changed the characters names, I lived every word of the story of this journey.

Publishing Date: 2014.05.01
http://www.melansonpublishing.com

On Mars: Vol 1. Pathfinder

This is my first full novel. It's a science fiction novel set on Mars. Our protagonist, every man Mike Lane goes alone on a proof of concept mission. Six minutes after landing, his landing craft explodes...

...then all hell breaks loose.

Fighting evil aliens, the environment and himself, Mike faces a struggle that was unexpected and that he's not totally unprepared for. Enter the beautiful alien hybrid woman who pledges that nothing will happen to him and things start to heat up.

Publishing Date: 2014.07.01
http://www.melansonpublishing.com
Please watch my site for information on when this new novel is published.

www.ingramcontent.com/pod-product-compliance
Lightning Source LLC
Chambersburg PA
CBHW060540030426
42337CB00021B/4362